Scratch   Table of Contents – 2017 Edit.

Learn tomorrow skills TODAY

with TomorrowSKILLS.COM

License Agreement

This book (the "Book") is a product provided by HobbyPRESS (being referred to as "HobbyPRESS" in this document), subject to your compliance with the terms and conditions set forth below. PLEASE READ THIS DOCUMENT CAREFULLY BEFORE ACCESSING OR USING THE BOOK. BY ACCESSING OR USING THE BOOK, YOU AGREE TO BE BOUND BY THE TERMS AND CONDITIONS SET FORTH BELOW. IF YOU DO NOT WISH TO BE BOUND BY THESE TERMS AND CONDITIONS, YOU MAY NOT ACCESS OR USE THE BOOK. HOBBYPRESS MAY MODIFY THIS AGREEMENT AT ANY TIME, AND SUCH MODIFICATIONS SHALL BE EFFECTIVE IMMEDIATELY UPON POSTING OF THE MODIFIED AGREEMENT ON THE CORPORATE SITE OF HOBBYPRESS. YOU AGREE TO REVIEW THE AGREEMENT PERIODICALLY TO BE AWARE OF SUCH MODIFICATIONS AND YOUR CONTINUED ACCESS OR USE OF THE BOOK SHALL BE DEEMED YOUR CONCLUSIVE ACCEPTANCE OF THE MODIFIED AGREEMENT.

Restrictions on Alteration

You may not modify the Book or create any derivative work of the Book or its accompanying documentation.   Derivative works include but are not limited to translations.

Restrictions on Copying

You may not copy any part of the Book unless formal written authorization is obtained from us.

Limitation of Liability

HobbyPRESS will not be held liable for any advice or suggestions given in this book. If the reader wants to follow a suggestion, it is at his or her own discretion. Suggestions are only offered to help.

IN NO EVENT WILL HOBBYPRESS BE LIABLE FOR (I) ANY INCIDENTAL, CONSEQUENTIAL, OR INDIRECT DAMAGES (INCLUDING, BUT NOT LIMITED TO, DAMAGES FOR LOSS OF PROFITS, BUSINESS INTERRUPTION, LOSS OF PROGRAMS OR INFORMATION, AND THE LIKE) ARISING OUT OF THE USE OF OR INABILITY TO USE THE BOOK. EVEN IF HOBBYPRESS OR ITS AUTHORIZED REPRESENTATIVES HAVE BEEN ADVISED OF THE POSSIBILITY OF SUCH DAMAGES, OR (II) ANY CLAIM ATTRIBUTABLE TO ERRORS, OMISSIONS, OR OTHER INACCURACIES IN THE BOOK. You agree to indemnify, defend and hold harmless HobbyPRESS, its officers, directors, employees, agents, licensors, suppliers and any third party information providers to the Book from and against all losses, expenses, damages and costs, including reasonable attorneys' fees, resulting from any violation of this Agreement (including negligent or wrongful conduct) by you or any other person using the Book.

Miscellaneous

This Agreement shall all be governed and construed in accordance with the laws of Hong Kong applicable to agreements made and to be performed in Hong Kong. You agree that any legal action or proceeding between HobbyPRESS and you for any purpose concerning this Agreement or the parties' obligations hereunder shall be brought exclusively in a court of competent jurisdiction sitting in Hong Kong.

About the TomorrowSKILLS Series

Give yourself a strong head start in computer programming with our TomorrowSKILLS books, which are published fresh in 2017. Through these books you will learn how programming works and how simple programs may be created using ready-made resources and modern drag-and-drop programming environments.

Basic Requirements

We assume you are totally new to programming. To make things easy for you, we use simple language throughout the book. And we simplify many of the technical terms into something more straight forward and human friendly. Most trade jargons are intentionally skipped.

This is an easy-read book that attempts to make concepts SIMPLE and STRAIGHTFORWARD. It does not aim to cover everything in Scratch. It simply tries to get you started quickly.

You need to be computer literate. You should know how to use a web browser since Scratch is web based. And you should have a reasonably configured computer system that comes with a dual core processor, 2GB+ of RAM, several GBs of free drive space that hold the resource files, and an active internet connection ... etc.

As of the time of this writing the latest version of Scratch is Scratch 2. It is available both online and offline. To use the online version, simply connect to: https://scratch.mit.edu and then click Create.

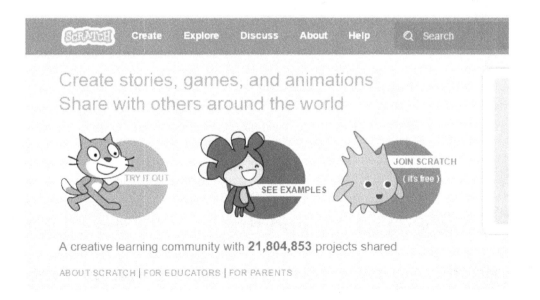

To use the offline version, download it from:

https://scratch.mit.edu/scratch2download/

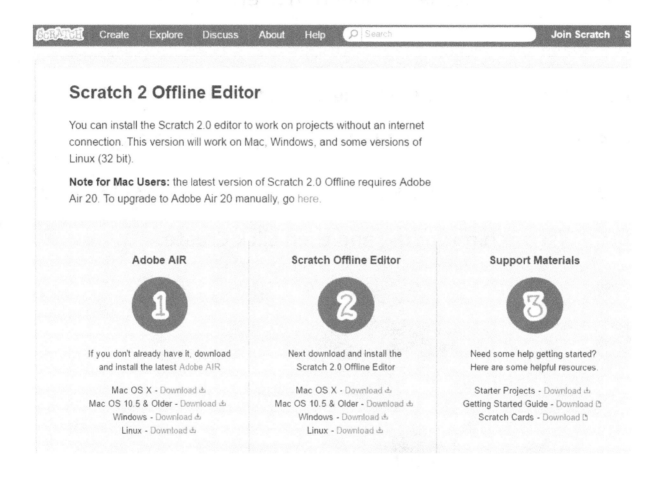

For simplicity sake we recommend that you use the online version. To do so you need a proper web browser. The latest version of Chrome is recommended.

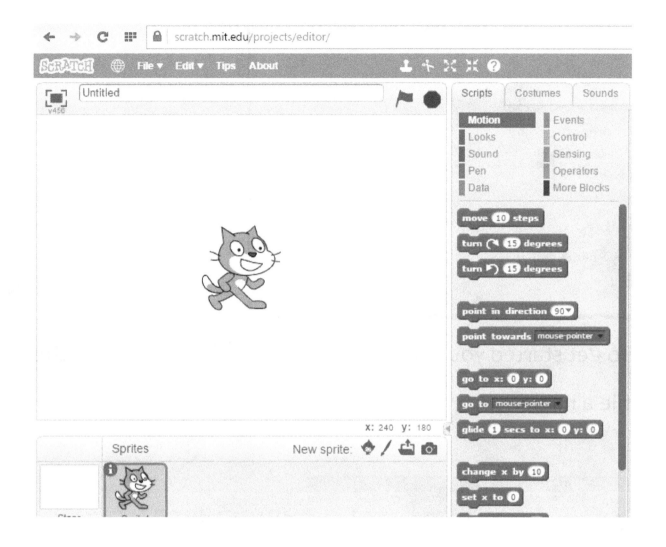

It is recommended that you first join Scratch so all the relevant settings can be retained even if you login from another location using another computer. It is free to join anyway.

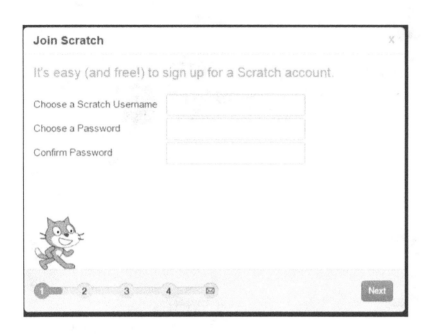

To get started you simply click File – New and then give the

file a name.

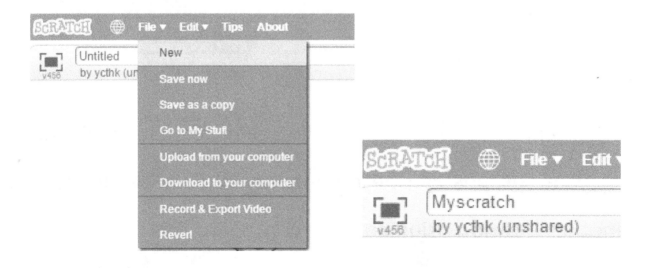

Every time you finish modifying something make sure you

download a copy of the project to your local computer!

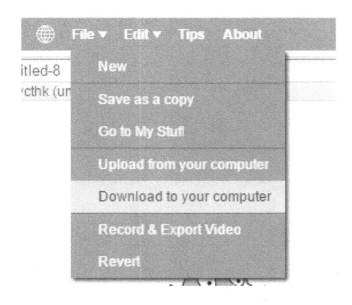

It is a SB2 file. You can always load it back into Scratch later via Upload from your computer.

Learning Goals

In a modern software development venture there are 3 different roles. Designers plan the program flow and conceptualize the various program features. Artists draw the user interface elements and the surrounding environment so to create the look and feel of the program. Programmers implement the design accordingly by writing codes. This book teaches you the basics of block based programming using Scratch. You will assume the role of a programmer and also a designer. And you will learn to use ready-made artworks from opensource to speed up the software creation process.

The Scratch interface allows you to code and then play the result directly. This is extremely useful for learning the essential programming concepts and logics:

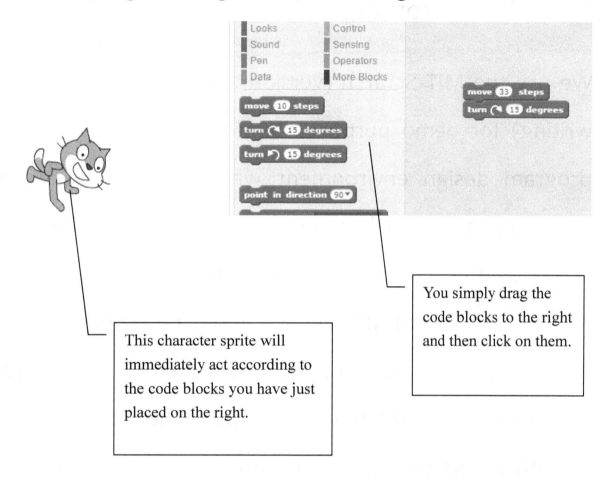

This character sprite will immediately act according to the code blocks you have just placed on the right.

You simply drag the code blocks to the right and then click on them.

Visual programming involves creating computer program using pictorial elements. Scratch is special in that apart from drag and drop it also offers a block mode – you drag and drop code blocks to form a program.

Tools and Resources

We use the MIT Scratch (version 2 as of the time of this writing) for demo purpose. Scratch is a drag and drop program design environment which also allows visual programming. Visual programming involves dragging "components". Simply put, you don't type codes - you drag and drop codes! Scratch is more for animation and game design. Its environment is extremely useful for learning purpose. It has 3 major panes. The stage pane on the left allows you to arrange the screen layout and the various character sprites. The code pane on the right allows you to code visually. The Sprite on the lower left is for working with sprite images.

Lesson 1 - the concept of sprite and stage

The first thing we want you to know is that everything that gets shown on screen is an object. The main character that you control is an object. The villains are enemy objects controlled by the computer. Tables, chairs, trees ... etc are all considered as objects. Sprites are the graphical representations of objects.

The stage is where the sprites are acting. After placing the necessary sprites on the stage, you define their basic behaviors through code blocks.

By default there is a cat sprite. You can choose to paint new sprite or upload sprite files from your computer.

It is good to have quality graphics and sound effects for enriching your game. OpenGameArt (http://opengameart.org) provides thousands of public domain game arts and sound effects that are completely free to use in your game.

Free artworks for games are typically offered as sprites and backdrops in JPG or PNG format. Sprites are for foreground objects while backdrops are for the background. They are usually made available in the form of sprite sheets so you can freely copy and paste.

Character sprites and tiles: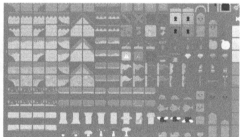

In Scratch, the default backdrop for the stage is plain white. Again, you can paint a new backdrop or upload a graphic file for it:

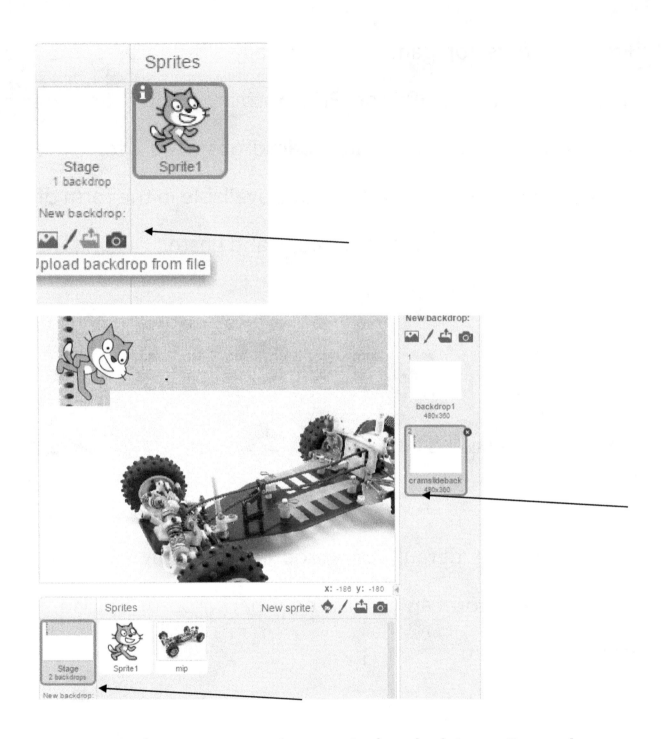

Do note that once an image is loaded into Scratch as a

Copyright 2017 **The HobbyPRESS (Hong Kong)**. All rights reserved.

sprite or a backdrop, you can immediately edit it using the

tools provided by the Costumes mode:

To resize the image, you can actually use a code block under the script mode:

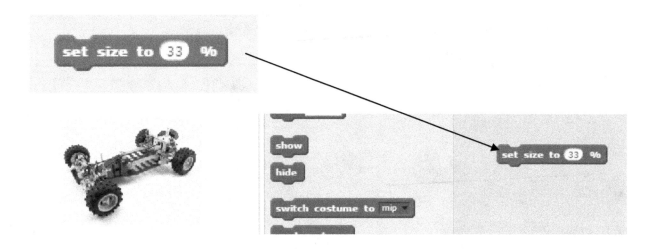

This is a flexible way of resizing a sprite – you can always adjust its size dynamically.

Lesson 1 con't – sprite and costume

A sprite can have one or more costumes, and you can always pick the costume for it.

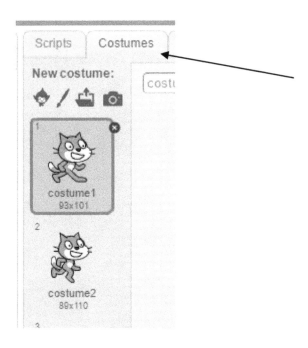

You can right click on a costume to duplicate or delete it.

Do realize that a costume is NOT a separate sprite!

If there is a need to save a costume to your computer,

right click on it and choose Save to local file. The file format is SVG, which is NOT a common image format.

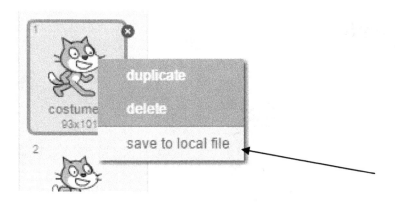

Copyright 2017 **The HobbyPRESS (Hong Kong)**.

Lesson 1 con't – manipulating sprites and backdrop programmatically

When there are multiple sprites, you can use your mouse to drag and move each sprite to the desired location on stage. If you need precise location and direction information of a sprite, navigate to Motion and check these items:

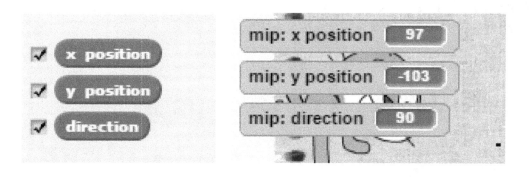

You can also set movement programmatically. Each sprite has its own set of code blocks (under Scripts). When you click on a sprite, you will only see the code blocks that belong to this particular sprite. You may pick the desired code block and drag it to the right pane. You can have as many code blocks as you like for a sprite. For testing purpose you do NOT have to plug all the blocks together. You can click on each individual block and see the individual effect produced. Or you may plug them together so they can function as a whole.

Looks deals with appearance while Motion deals with movement:

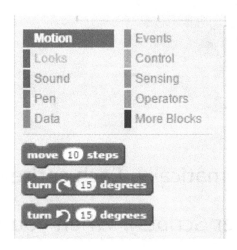

To set its direction using an absolute value, use:

To rotate it (in other words, every rotation is done relative to the present direction), use:

To move it (in the unit of steps) following the current direction, use:

Keep in mind, move XX steps would only go forward the direction your sprite is facing! To set its precise X and Y position, use:

It is recommended that you try these code blocks out and see how they work.

When one object runs into another so they overlap, you can use these Looks go blocks to move an object upfront or to the back. "Layers" is like a stack, when you have multiple objects overlapping, you have multiple layers stacking up.

You may also dynamically show and hide a sprite using these:

Copyright 2017 **The HobbyPRESS (Hong Kong)**.

To programmatically switch costume for a sprite, use this code block:

Although you cannot move a backdrop around, you can switch to a different backdrop programmatically:

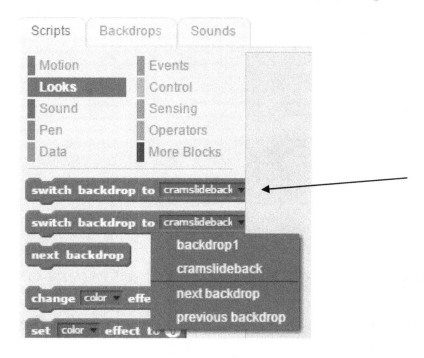

Backdrop always stays at the back. It would not collide with any of the sprites.

Lesson 1 con't – screen coordinates

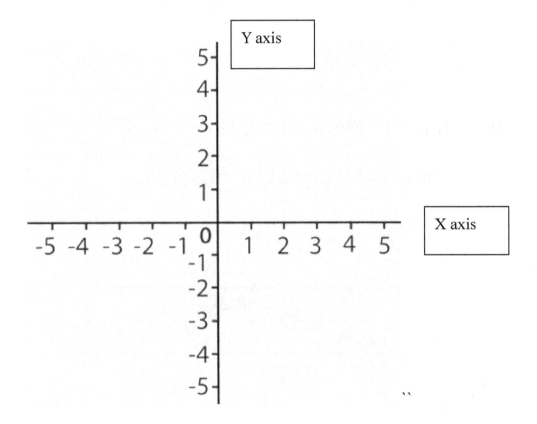

On a 2D screen, the coordinates are based on a system of X and Y. This system is known as the Cartesian coordinate system, which has a pair of lines on a flat surface that intersect at right angles.   The lines are axes and the point at which they intersect is the origin.   The axes are laid horizontally and vertically and are known as the x-axis and y-axis respectively.

A point with coordinates X and Y is X units to the right of the y axis and Y units up from the x axis. It is possible for them to carry negative values. For Scratch, just keep these in mind:

• When X increases, the sprite is moving to the right, and vice versa.

• When Y increases, the sprite is moving upward, and vice versa.

Lesson 2 - accepting and processing user input

Different platforms accept different inputs. With Scratch, the most popular user input formats are mouse click and keyboard key press (they all belong to Events). You simply need to tie an input event to a particular sprite object. For example, you want the cat to say hello to you when it is clicked. These are the code blocks to use:

If you want the cat to rotate 90 degrees to the right and

say Hi when the spacebar (or any other key) is pressed, use these code blocks:

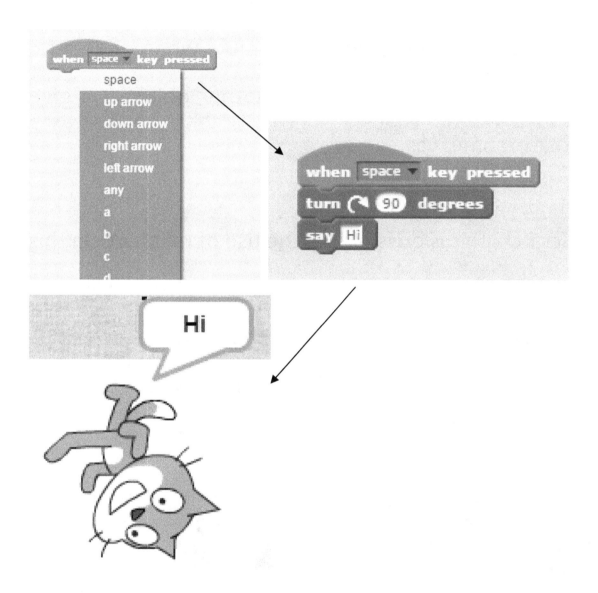

Copyright 2017 **The HobbyPRESS (Hong Kong)**. All rights reserved.

Lesson 2 con't – object interaction via messages

A program is all about interactions among objects! What we want you to achieve here is simple – when one sprite object is receiving a user input, another object will give response in some way.

With Scratch, this is possible via the use of message. In this example, when the green flag receives a click, it will send out a message openly. Then when the kicker receives this message, it will rotate itself. First you need to set the code blocks for the cat:

Then you need to set the code blocks for the kicker sprite:

The so called message1 does not have any content. It is kind of like a signal. You can click New message to define more messages for the sprites to interact differently.

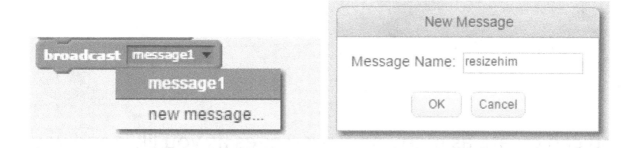

This time when the cat itself receives a click, it will send out the new "resizehim" message. The kicker will accordingly resize himself after a 3-second delay.

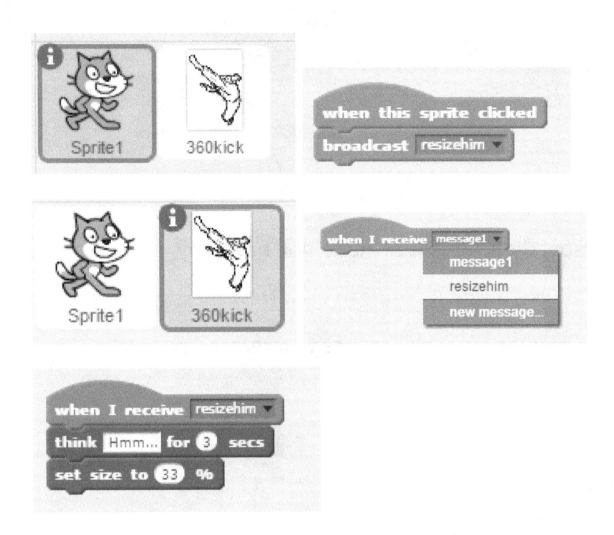

You can create as many new messages as you like, and you can name these messages freely. As previously said, they are just signal - the meaning of the name doesn't matter.

Lesson 2 con't – collision detection

When a sprite object is in touch with another, a collision occurs. In the context of Scratch, this is being referred to as a touch.

Refer to this code block:

When the cat is clicked, it will move for 10 steps. If it touches the kicker sprite, it will turn for 55 degrees.

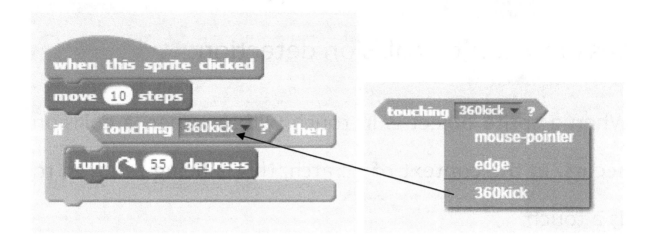

The touching code block belongs to Sensing (you can choose what target to sense for). On the other hand, the If then block that holds the touch block belongs to Control.

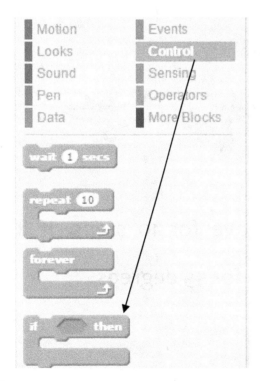

Lesson 3 – if then else logic

In the previous lesson there is a IF block. You need this to implement logical choices. IF THEN is the most basic of all the control flow statements. It basically tells the program to execute a certain action (or a series of actions) only if a particular condition is evaluated to true. ELSE provides a secondary alternative path of execution when the IF condition evaluates to false.

To summarize:

- IF THEN - IF some condition is true, perform an action; otherwise do nothing.

- IF THEN ELSE - IF some condition is true, perform an action; otherwise (ELSE) perform a different action.

You use IF THEN when there is no alternative action. When there is alternative action, you will need to use ELSE. The condition to evaluate can be found under Sensing. Here is an example:

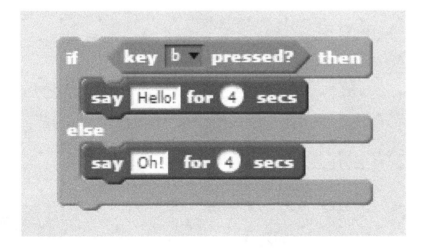

Copyright   2017   **The HobbyPRESS (Hong Kong)**.

It basically says when the b key is pressed the cat will say Hello for 4 seconds, otherwise it will say "Oh!" instead.

If you have several IF THEN blocks and you plan them correctly, they may function exactly the same as having multiple ELSEs... Just remember, the evaluation would always go from top to bottom (i.e. sequentially).

Lesson 3 con't – and VS or

If the condition to evaluate has multiple elements that must exist together (AND) or individually (OR), you need to make use of the blocks under Operators. These blocks can be plugged into the IF THEN block for defining multiple conditions.

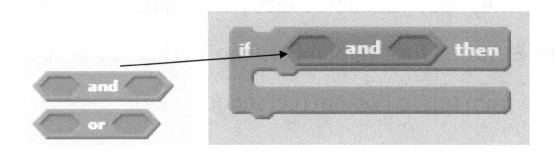

For example, to allow the cat to scream when both the a key and the b key are pressed:

To test this block, you first press and hold both keys then click on the block.

If you use a OR block, then pressing either key will work.

Lesson 3 con't – nesting if then else logics

You can make the entire logic more advanced:

- if both keys are pressed the cat will scream and rotate

- if only one key is pressed cat will rotate but not scream

You can do this by nesting two blocks together. Nesting means having one type of instruction within another. It is technically okay to have one or more IF/THEN/ELSE instructions within other IF/THEN/ELSE instructions. HOWEVER, when nesting goes too deep a level the entire block can become quite confusing to read and interpret.

In this example we only nest one block within another.

Copyright   2017   **The HobbyPRESS (Hong Kong)**.

```
if < <key [a ▾] pressed?> and <key [b ▾] pressed?> > then
    turn ↻ (44) degrees
else

```

```
if < <key [a ▾] pressed?> or <key [b ▾] pressed?> > then
    play sound [meow ▾]
    turn ↻ (44) degrees
```

```
if < <key [a ▾] pressed?> and <key [b ▾] pressed?> > then
    turn ↻ (44) degrees
else
    if < <key [a ▾] pressed?> or <key [b ▾] pressed?> > then
        play sound [meow ▾]
        turn ↻ (44) degrees
```

For this nesting attempt to be logically correct, you need to allow the AND condition to run first. If you let the OR condition go first, the AND condition will never be met. This is because when you press both keys together, logically it would already have met the a OR b condition!

Lesson 3 con't – other ways to manage the flow of the program

There are two code blocks that may be useful. Wait allows you to set the program to pause for a number of seconds programmatically. Stop allows you to selectively stop the execution of certain scripts. This will be particularly useful if the player needs to stop the game abruptly.

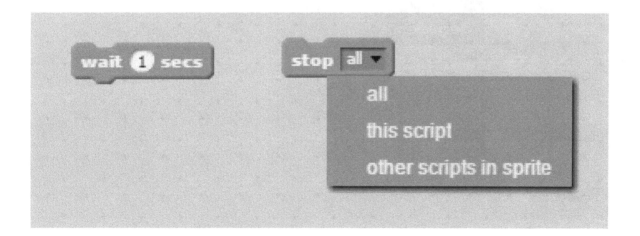

With Wait you need to predefine the number of seconds to wait. If you are not sure about the duration to wait, use

Wait Until instead. This allows you to define a condition for the wait.

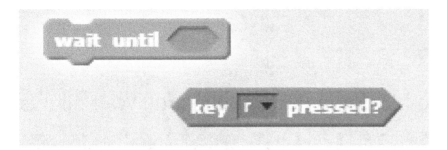

To try out the effect of the wait blocks you should test them out like this:

move 55 steps
wait 3 secs
turn ↻ 33 degrees
move 55 steps
wait until key r ▼ pressed?
turn ↻ 33 degrees
move 55 steps

Lesson 3 con't – the green flag

You can click on a certain code block to run it. If you want to run all the code blocks together, you need to rely on the green flag. This Green Flag when clicked will start all scripts in that project equipped with the When Green Flag Clicked block:

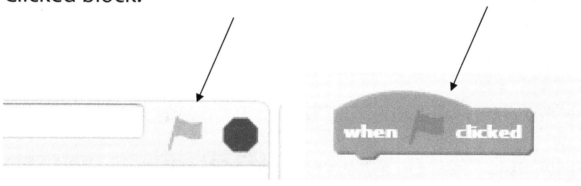

The Stop Sign next to the flag is for stopping all the running scripts.

Lesson 4 - loop

A very important control logic you need to know is loop. A loop basically repeats things until a particular condition is met. A repeat loop is the most common form of loop in Scratch.

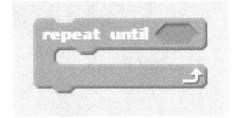

The code block allows you to repeat some actions until a condition is met. An easy example - repeat until the space bar is pressed:

Say you want the cat to keep moving to the right until the

space bar is pressed. This time the "change x by ..." block is used inside the repeat loop. Change x means changing the x position of the sprite.

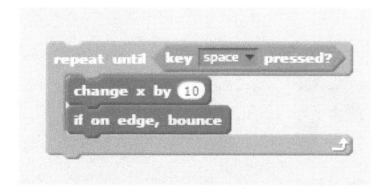

With this code block, the change X action is being repeated and repeated. If space bar is not pressed, the cat will soon hit the right end of the screen and get stuck over there. You may add a bounce action to the block accordingly...

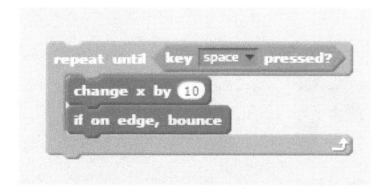

Another very important loop is the Forever loop. This is a loop with no condition. It just keeps running forever. You will find it very useful for "listening" to user inputs (we will talk about this later)

Lesson 4 con't – implementing movement control

To implement movement control so that the sprite can move according to the keys pressed, you will need to use a combination of code blocks.

The following key functions are planned:

s pressed – the sprite will change from a cat to a buggy

u pressed – move up

d pressed – move down

r pressed – move to the right

l pressed – move to the left

To implement s, first you import a new image into costume:

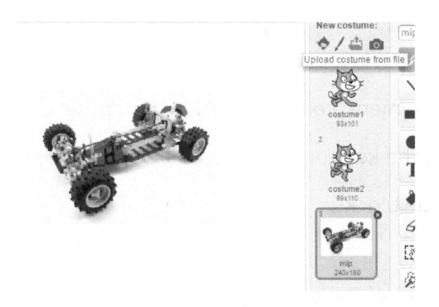

Then you have this block ready:

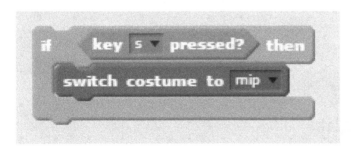

To implement u, you need these code blocks assembled together (this becomes a little more complicated):

You need the program to keep listening to user inputs.
This is why you need a Forever loop. Then if u is pressed,
the repeat loop will start which involves changing the Y
position of the sprite 10 at a time. This will keep going until
u is NO LONGER pressed. The NOT block belongs to
Operators.

Now you need to implement the rest (it is better to

organize these blocks step by step):

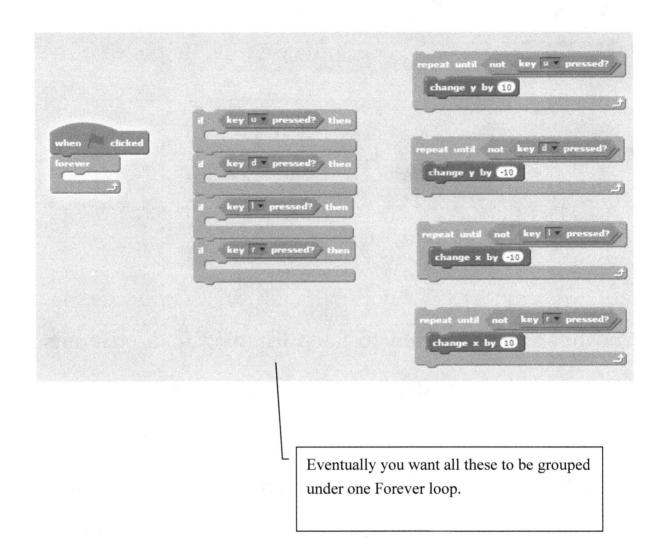

Eventually you want all these to be grouped under one Forever loop.

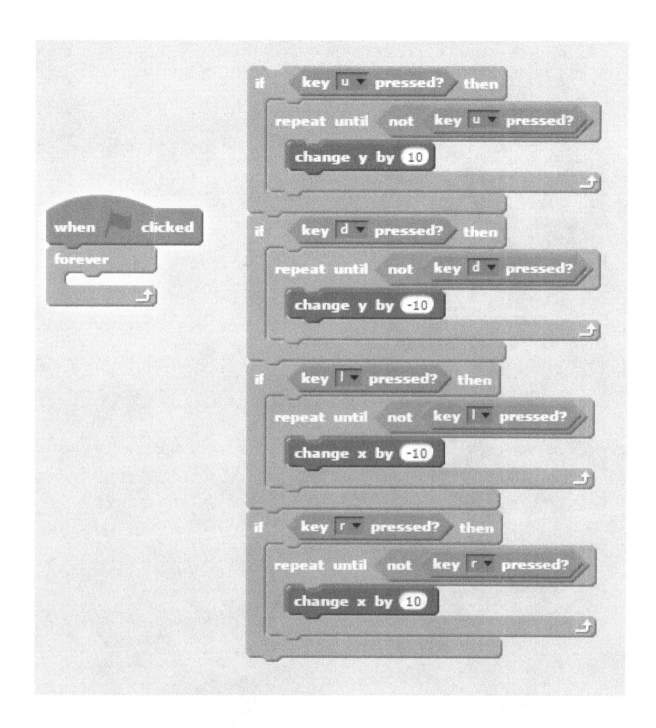

Copyright 2017 **The HobbyPRESS (Hong Kong)**. All rights reserved.

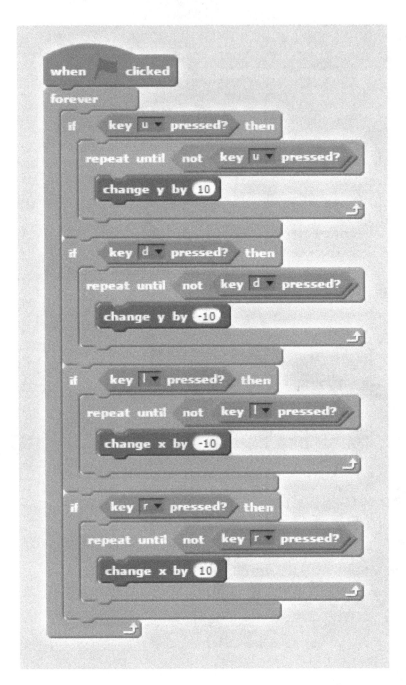

And finally you want the s pressed block to be included as well...

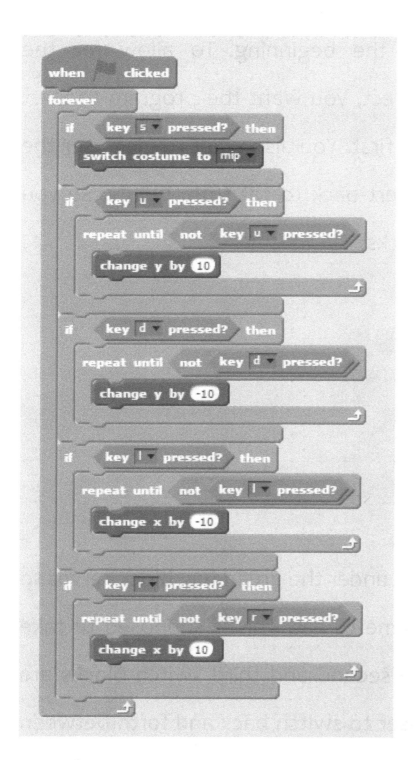

There is one issue here – the sprite starts with the buggy

costume right from the beginning. To allow for the changing costume effect, you want the program to start with the cat costume first. You also want to give user the ability to later on revert back to cat from buggy. So you need to add these blocks:

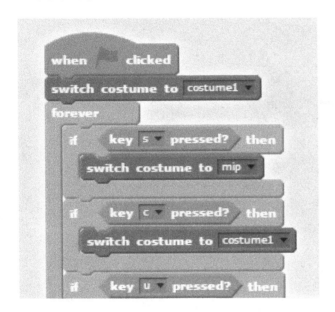

The switch block right under the green flag block serves to set the default costume to cat. This is supposed to take place once only. The second and third switch blocks are inside the loop for user to switch back and forth between cat and buggy. They need to stay inside the loop so the program can constantly listen to them.

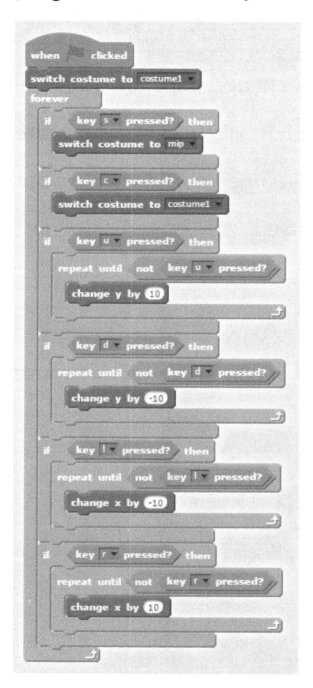

Lesson 5 – manipulating variables

A variable is a value that can change depending on the conditions encountered. Scratch allows you to create variables that are not visible – in other words, they are not components that are displayed on screen but just "something" behind the scene.

Under Data there is a Make a variable button you can use to create new variables.

The variable can be public (ie. it works for all sprites) or private (i.e. it is specific to the current sprite only). You are going to create 2 variables representing the location max height and max width of the screen area. For simplicity sake just keep them public. When you create them, some very useful code blocks are automatically made available by Scratch.

A newly created variable has no value by default so you need to give it a default value (ie. initialize them) using the

Set _____ to block. This block should run once only so it should stay outside of the Forever loop.

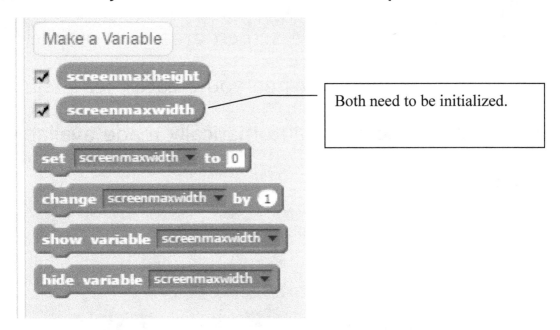

Both need to be initialized.

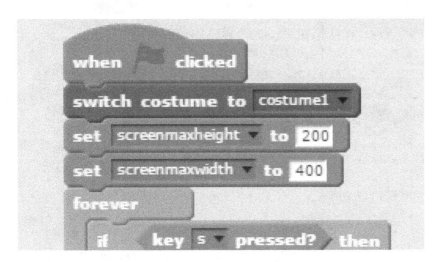

Now you need to setup a mechanism so that when the

sprite moves out of these boundaries it will be sent back to somewhere around the middle of the screen. You need to first construct the relevant IF THEN logic using these blocks.

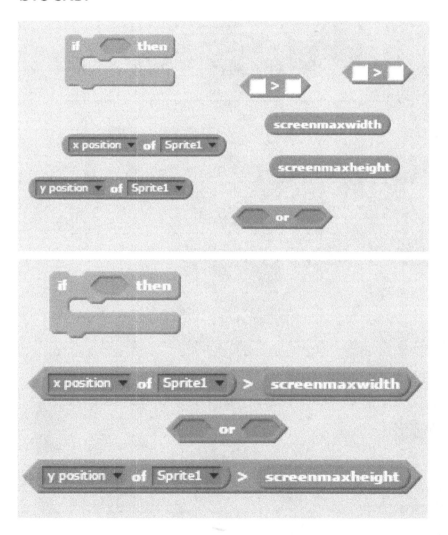

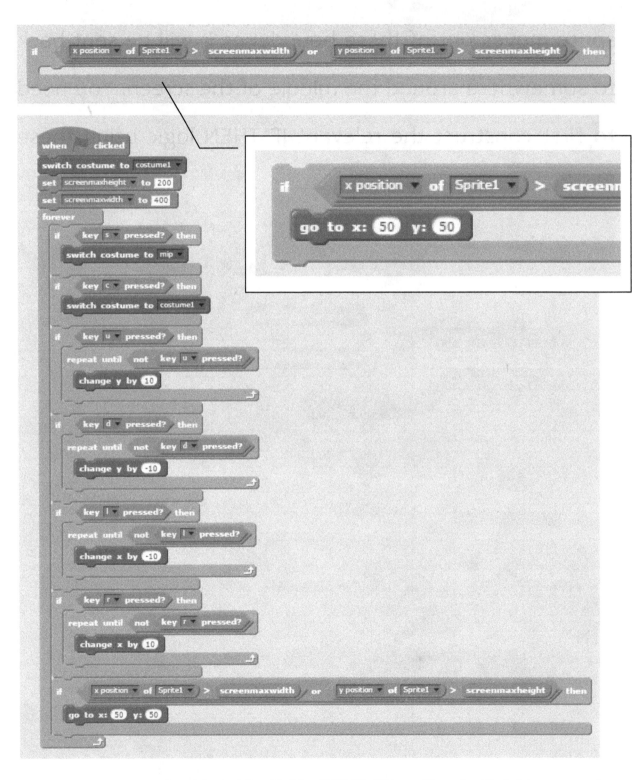

To do the same when the sprite moves too low or too left (below x = 0 and y = 0), use these blocks:

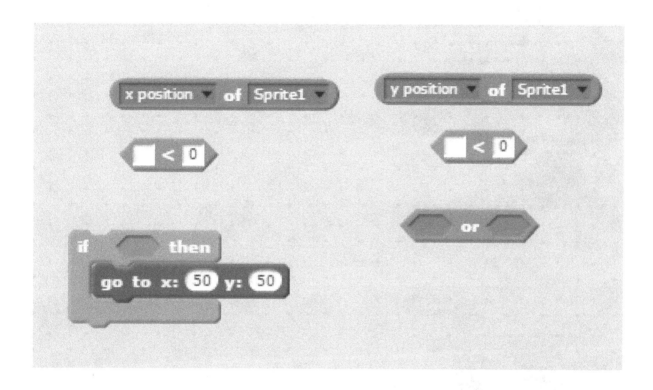

```
when clicked
switch costume to costume1
set screenmaxheight to 200
set screenmaxwidth to 400
forever
    if key s pressed? then
        switch costume to mip
    if key c pressed? then
        switch costume to costume1
    if key u pressed? then
        repeat until not key u pressed?
            change y by 10
    if key d pressed? then
        repeat until not key d pressed?
            change y by -10
    if key l pressed? then
        repeat until not key l pressed?
            change x by -10
    if key r pressed? then
        repeat until not key r pressed?
            change x by 10
    if x position of Sprite1 > screenmaxwidth or y position of Sprite1 > screenmaxheight then
        go to x: 50 y: 50
    if x position of Sprite1 < 0 or y position of Sprite1 < 0 then
        go to x: 50 y: 50
```

Now you have learned the basics. When you are ready to move on, please try out our Game Creation Starter books at http://gameengines.net.

END OF BOOK

Please email your questions and comments to admin@Tomorrowskills.com.

www.ingramcontent.com/pod-product-compliance
Lightning Source LLC
Chambersburg PA
CBHW060206060326
40690CB00018B/4276